Apple in the Woods

By

Tina M. Fournier

Apple in the Woods

Published by Isabella Media Inc doing business as Isabella's Book Club

270 Bellevue Ave #1002, Newport RI 02840

www.IsabellasBookClub.com

ISBN-13: 978-1735725666

For permissions contact: requests@isabellamedia.com

Once upon a time, there was a dog named Apple. She enjoyed adventures deep, deep, into the woods where fairies and talking bushes lived.

Apple is a fun-loving dog who looks a little different than most dogs; she has one ear that sticks straight up and one ear that flops over.

One day while Apple was deep, deep into the woods, a fairy named Erika brightened her day. "Hello!" she said.

The happy and playful fairy twinkled around Apple's nose singing and dancing. With a smile, she asked Apple, "Would you like to sing and dance with me?"

Apple was excited to make a new friend, "Yes! I would like to very much!" she replied. Apple and Erika danced around the woods, having a great time together.

Suddenly Erika stopped singing and hovered in the air quietly. Apple was still dancing until she realized Erika had stopped. Apple turned around to see that not too far away, a bush had grabbed Erika's attention.

Deep, deep in the woods, there are bushes that can talk... and boy, can they talk! But this bush was fast asleep. But even though it was sleeping, it was moving. Something was hiding in the bush! Apple and Erika walked over to the bush to see about this mystery .

All of a sudden, a cat leaped out of the bush! Apple and Erika were not expecting anything to jump out at them. The cat scared them. They both fell onto their tooshies. The cat laughed so hard it fell onto its tooshie too.

Apple and Erika got up and went over to the cat, and asked what his name was. The cat replied, “My name is Josh.” Then Josh looked at Apple in a very odd way.

"What's wrong?" Apple asked.

Josh replied, "Your ears are the coolest ears I have ever seen! I wish I had ears like that."

"Thank you," Apple replied with a smile.

The grey dog with cool-looking ears introduced Erika, the tiny fairy, to Josh the cat. Josh asked if he could join them in their singing and dancing adventure. They agreed and continued to the pond. They were excited to arrive at the pond, where they were sure to meet some cute, funny, and mysterious creatures.

After singing and dancing to a few songs. Josh asked, "How much farther is the pond?"

Erika replied, "We just need to pass where the horseshoe meets the hat. Then we will be there."

The cat thought for a minute, then asked, "Horseshoe meets the hat? How far away is that? We have been dancing around for a long time. And where is there a horseshoe or hat in the middle of the woods?"

Apple laughed, "Look at that rock next to the oak tree. It is shaped like a hat. Look at the old horn lying on the ground next to it. It looks like a horseshoe. We are here."

"Here at the pond?" Josh asked, "I don't see a pond."

"If you just close your eyes for a couple of seconds and imagine a pond, it will be there," Apple said. "Deep, deep in the woods is a magical place."

Josh closed his eyes and imagined a beautiful pond with ducks, swans, and butterflies flying around. When he opened his eyes, he was amazed by what he saw. He saw exactly what he imagined. There was a pond with ducks swimming with their families, beautiful swans by the edge, and endless amounts of butterflies fluttering around. One of them stopped and landed on the tip of his nose, making him wiggle it. There was even a couple of Elves diving in the water.

Josh could barely believe his cat eyes. He was standing in front of a pond that wasn't there before he imagined it. This was truly a magical place.

Apple ran and jumped into the pond, and Erika flew over everything from edge to edge.

Josh just stood there watching. He was nervous but wanted to have fun too. But he was embarrassed because he didn't know how to swim.

"Come in and play!" Apple yelled to him.

Erika flew over to Josh and told him to go ahead and jump in. She told him not to worry, that this was a magical place where no one ever got hurt.

"The pond will protect you. You will float, and the pond will help you learn to swim." Erika said.

Josh thought that sounded silly. How could a pond show him how to swim?

Now fairies are pretty small, but Erika swooped down, and before Josh knew it, he was being picked and dropped into the pond. Then, Erika flew down and dove into the water next to him. Josh was scared and started splashing all over the place until he realized he was floating. Then he started to move through the pond, kicking with his back and front paws. "I am swimming!" Josh said with excitement.

All Josh needed was a little nudge from Erika to help him overcome his fear and to learn. She wanted to help him, not laugh at him because he didn't know how to swim. Josh had made some wonderful new friends.

Apple, Erika, and Josh played in the pond all afternoon. They were having so much fun that they didn't realize how late it was getting.

Once out of the pond, they realized how hungry they were. Their bellies were making rumbling sounds. They said goodbye to the ducks, swans, butterflies, and Elves and went in search of a snack. They started walking, but Erika flew ahead and soon came back, fluttering her wings with excitement. She told them that there were strawberry bushes ahead next to some pretty trees and logs that they could sit on.

The cool-looking eared dog, cat, and fairy plucked berries from bushes and sat on the logs. They ate till their bellies were full. Each of them with a big grin on their faces, happy for the new friends they made.

The End

CPSIA information can be obtained
at www.ICGtesting.com
Printed in the USA
BVHW021908081221
623568BV00002B/7

* 9 7 8 1 7 3 5 7 2 5 6 6 6 *